Drake Montana is an explorer and naturalist who has traveled all over the world. He observes animals in their natural environment and records their behavior in his journal. He is traveling with his assistant Max and a mountain climbing guide named Jade.

DRAKE

MAX

JADE

K & M International
1955 Midway Drive
Twinsburg, Ohio 44087

First Edition
Printed in Hong Kong
ISBN - 1-890716-08-1

Contributing writer, Bob Kaminski

The Adventures of
Drake Montana
Asian Mountains

A K & M International Publication

Illustrated by
Jason Karecki

It is the middle of the afternoon on this cold January day. Drake, Max and Jade have moved their camp to the foot of the Himalayan Mountains where they are tracking a snow leopard. This expedition has introduced them to a variety of animals along the way that they did not expect to see. They settled on a ledge for a break from climbing and Drake reviewed his journal.

January 6: We boarded a plane for Asia, where we hope to observe the elusive snow leopard.

SNOW LEOPARD

- The snow leopard lives in caves and cracks high in the Himalayan Mountains.
- The thick hair around the snow leopard's paws cushion its feet from the rough rocks and allow it to walk over snow without sinking.
- The snow leopard hunts alone, preying on blue sheep, ibexes, wild goats, hares, birds and mice.
- The snow leopard's eyes are positioned high on its head to allow it to hide while stalking its prey.

This expedition will require the very difficult task of climbing the Himalayan mountains in China, but I am looking forward to the challenge.

January 7: Soon after our expedition started we made an emergency landing in Honshu, Japan. It seems we had lost the use of one of our two engines. Because it will take a few days to fix the problem, we decided to set out to observe some of the wildlife of the Japan Alps.

HONSHU, JAPAN

After hiking many miles we noticed several monkeys called Japanese macaques sitting on the ground hugging each other to keep warm.

JAPANESE MACAQUE

- Japanese macaques live in groups of 20 to 100 monkeys.
- In addition to relying on each other for warmth, these monkeys have thick fur.
- The Japanese macaque is an excellent climber and swimmer.

After a short time, the group of macaques made its way to the hot springs and eased into the water. They relaxed as the heat from the water warmed their bodies.

January 10: Finally, our plane was ready. We boarded the plane and flew across the Sea of Japan to the Yunnan Region of China. While we refueled, we took a walk to stretch our legs. During our walk we witnessed a water monitor rushing down a tree and into the water.

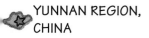

YUNNAN REGION,
CHINA

WATER MONITOR

- The water monitor lives in waterfront areas, where it can swim and climb trees.
- It eats snakes, frogs and birds.
- It is a close relative to the world's largest lizard, the komodo dragon.

January 11: We arrived at the Hengduan Mountains in western China. After several days of searching, we finally saw a large greater panda feasting on some bamboo. It was using the extra thumb on its forepaws to grab the very small bamboo shoots.

GREATER PANDA

- The greater panda can weigh up to 265 pounds and stand 5 feet tall.
- Its waterproof coat of fur allows it to survive in the cold, damp areas where it lives.
- Its paws have long, retractable claws.
- The greater panda feeds mostly on bamboo, which has little nutritional value. As a result, it spends 16 hours a day eating 25 to 45 pounds of bamboo to keep its stomach full.

January 14: Max discovered a red panda sleeping with its front and back paws wrapped around a tree branch. He barely noticed it because the brown color of its fur blended in with the tree. The red panda actually looks more like a raccoon than a panda.

RED PANDA

- The red panda is a close relative of the greater panda.
- Also called the "lesser" panda, the red panda can weigh up to 14 pounds and stand 2 feet tall.
- Like the greater panda, it has an extra thumb on both of its forepaws and it feeds mostly on bamboo. The red panda also eats small birds, mammals and reptiles.
- The red panda is an excellent climber and can jump 5 feet from branch to branch.
- The red panda is more active at night. It spends most of the day resting and sleeping in trees.

TIBET

January 15: We left the Hengduan Mountains and flew to the Himalayas. As we landed, I saw a number of ibexes climbing along the rocky cliffs.

Two males charged each other, ramming the huge horns on their heads together. It is amazing how they keep their balance.

IBEX

- The ibex is a type of wild goat.
- It has split hooves, which help it climb hills and rocks. It rarely slips or falls.
- Both males and females have a pair of horns that curve out of the tops of their heads. Males have longer, heavier horns. The length of its horns indicates how old an ibex is.

Just then, a few falling pebbles startled Drake. Looking up from his journal, he was excited to see a snow leopard leaping from one rock to another.

Drake, Max and Jade grew nervous as they noticed the snow leopard moving closer and closer towards them. They left their rest site and slowly backed away along the ledge, always keeping an eye on the snow leopard. For every 15 to 20 feet that they walked, the snow leopard moved to a rock just above them, as if it was preparing for an attack. Drake, Max and Jade were sure they would see a snow leopard hunt on this expedition, but they had no idea that they might end up being the prey.

To their surprise, an ibex suddenly darted out from behind them. The snow leopard jumped down from the rock and chased the ibex. Drake, Max and Jade watched until the two animals were out of sight.

After tracking the snow leopard for several days, Drake, Max and Jade returned to their camp, where Drake and Max prepared for their next expedition to the Pacific Ocean. They thanked Jade for her help and she wished them luck on their next adventure.

GLOSSARY TERMS

Darted – A quick movement.
Elusive – To escape without notice.
Tracked – To follow the tracks of an animal.
Waterproof – Resistant to water.